BRITISH RAILWAYS

PAST and PRESENT

No 30

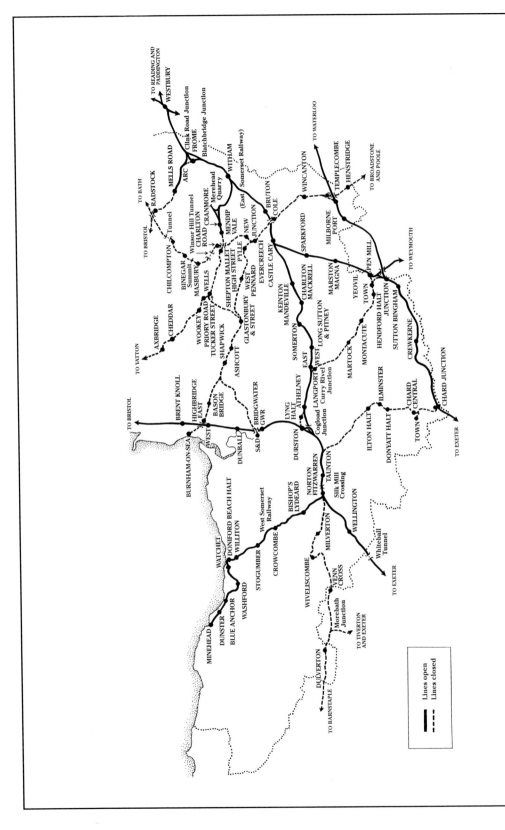

BRITISH RAILWAYS

PAST and PRESENT

No 30

Somerset

David Mitchell

Past and Present

Past & Present Publishing Ltd

First published in November 1996

British Library Cataloguing in Publication Data

A catalogue record for this book is available from the British Library

ISBN 1 85895 088 0

Past & Present Publishing Ltd
Unit 5
Home Farm Close
Church Street
Wadenhoe
Peterborough PE8 5TE
Tel (01832) 720440/531
Fax (01832) 720531
e-mail: pete@slinkp-p.demon.co.uk

Maps drawn by Christina Siviter

Printed and bound in Great Britain

SHEPTON MALLET (CHARLTON ROAD): The much-loved and lamented Somerset & Dorset Railway features in these pages, but any recollections that steam days were always accompanied by long hot summers are disproved somewhat by this view as S&D 2-8-0 No 53807 passes through the station with a Nottingham to Bournemouth West train on a rather wet 21 July 1962.

In comparison, there was plenty of sunshine in the summer of 1995, but unfortunately not such attractive subject matter was available for the cameraman! *Roy Lumber/DHM*

CONTENTS

BIBLIOGRAPHY

Regional History of the Railways of Great Britain, Vol 1 The West Country *by David St John Thomas (David & Charles)*

The Railways of Bristol & Somerset *by Martin Smith (Ian Allan)*

Atlas of the GWR *by R. A. Cooke (Wild Swan)*

Track Layout Diagrams of the GWR, Sections 9, 15 to 18, and 21 *by R. A. Cooke*

An Historical Survey of the Somerset & Dorset *by C. W. Judge & C. R. Potts (OPC)*

The Somerset & Dorset Then & Now *by Mac Hawkins (PSL)*

Through Countryside and Coalfield *by Mike Vincent (OPC)*

The Story of the Westbury to Weymouth Line *by Derek Phillips (OPC)*

Working Yeovil to Taunton Steam *by Derek Phillips (Fox & Co)*

Working the Chard Branch *by Derek Phillips & R. Eaton-Lacey (Fox & Co)*

Albums by Vic Mitchell and Keith Smith (Middleton Press)
  Burnham to Evercreech Junction
  Bournemouth to Evercreech Junction
  Bath to Evercreech Junction
  Frome to Bristol
  Salisbury to Yeovil
  Yeovil to Exeter
  Branch Line to Minehead
  Taunton to Barnstaple

INTRODUCTION

Somerset is an attractive and largely unspoilt county devoid of any major urban conurbations. Within its relatively narrow confines it has a magnificently varied landscape with the limestone Mendip Hills marking its northern boundary. South of these lie the wide expense of the levels, while the sandstone hill ranges of the west culminate in the delights of the Exmoor National Park.

The coming of the railway to the area was initiated by a group of Bristol merchants who promoted the Bristol & Exeter, which opened as far as Bridgwater in 1841. It was engineered by Brunel and built to his broad gauge. Originally it was leased to the Great Western Railway, then after a subsequent period of independence it was absorbed by the GWR, which had by then already taken over the Wilts, Somerset & Weymouth Railway. The B&E had also fostered the Somerset Central, and potentially the broad gauge could have completely dominated the county's railway network.

However, when the London & South Western Railway extended from Salisbury, its route westwards was to take it through the south of the county, and standard gauge interests were further enhanced when the Somerset Central amalgamated with the LSWR-worked Dorset Central to form the Somerset & Dorset Railway. After a series of financial crises, the S&D was leased jointly to the LSWR and the Midland Railway, and its unique history has no doubt contributed towards the legendary status that it has acquired in recent years.

The county's railway system was thus to become almost as diverse as its landscape, not only in the wide range of motive power and rolling-stock, but also in the different architectural styles adopted by the various companies. It is hoped that some flavour of this can be gleaned when perusing these pages.

Somerset lost the northerly third of its area in 1974 when the new county of Avon was created. This portion has already been included in volume No 16 of this series and is thus excluded from this book. Also, until 1995 the station at Yeovil Junction was located within Dorset, and has accordingly received extensive coverage in volume No 29.

Within the current county boundaries it is sad to report that the railway system is now a pale shadow of its former self. Although the main lines remain open, many of the intermediate stations have closed, and today the preserved West Somerset Railway can offer as many stops as that provided on all of Railtrack's metals! The South Western and Great Western services were the first to be franchised under the current privatisation process and the remaining stations served by these companies receive a fairly good level of service.

The route from Castle Cary to Yeovil and south to Weymouth has also happily survived the years of retrenchment, but unfortunately the other secondary routes and all of the passenger branch lines have long since been closed. Holiday resorts such as Burnham and Minehead owe much to the railway for their development, but now have to rely on road transport for their summer visitors.

Industry in the county has been based traditionally on agriculture, and produce from Somerset's rich pastures once provided much welcome income for the railway. However, it

CROGUMBER station's cramped location on the side of a valley can be noted on 24 August 1963 as BR Standard Prairie tank No 82042 leaves on the 12.07 pm Minehead to Cardiff train. A camping coach stands next to the cattle dock on the right, this being a feature of the station from the 1930s until 1964.

The goods shed has been demolished, but otherwise today's scene is not too different. On 5 May 1996 ex-LMS 0-6-0 No 44422 departs with the 14.00 Minehead-Bishop's Lydeard service. The '4F' was on loan from the North Staffordshire Railway and as a former Somerset & Dorset engine was an appropriate visitor to the county. *Peter Gray/DHM*

7

also benefited from a surprisingly diverse range of other activities, whether it was peat-digging on the levels, quarrying in the Mendips or even coal-mining in the north of the county.

Today the picture is not such a happy one, although at the time of writing there are prospects of milk returning to the rails, and it is to be hoped that the positive approach being adopted by the newly privatised English, Welsh & Scottish freight operation may lead to other traffic, including cider from Taunton, also being regained. Apart from the nuclear flasks handled at Bridgwater, there are currently only two other sources of revenue-earning freight in Somerset, but these are certainly notable with substantial flows emanating from the giant aggregate quarries operated by Foster Yeoman and ARC in the Mendips. The former were enterprising pioneers when in 1986 they were the first company to purchase their own locomotives for use on BR metals. The success of their General Motors Class 59 was such that their rivals followed suit, and to maximise efficiency the companies have since combined their resources to form the Mendip Rail operation.

The county has much to offer the steam enthusiast, with two preserved lines operating within its boundaries. After troubled beginnings when it was beset by financial difficulties and was being operated by inadequate motive power, the West Somerset is now a thriving concern and major tourist attraction. It is the longest private line in the country, and a journey beside the Quantock Hills and along the Bristol Channel coast is a splendid way to enjoy Somerset's glorious scenery. The East Somerset, based at Cranmore, is a smaller affair, but in its own way is also successful in recreating something of the steam age. Both lines retain links with the national network, which allows special trains to visit them.

This is the fourth volume in this series that I have been involved in compiling, and once again I must express my thanks to the 'past' photographers who have provided not only excellent archive material, but have also responded to my requests for further information each is individually credited in the book. Prints of photographs from the Mowat Collection can be obtained from W. R. Burton, 3 Fairway, Clifton, York. Thanks also go to Eric Youldon for his comments on the manuscript, and especially to the land-owners who kindly allowed me access to their property.

David Mitchell
Exeter

The Bristol & Exeter

BRENT KNOLL: The village is named after the nearby hill that rises to an altitude of 450 feet above the Somerset levels. Its station opened in 1875 and is pictured here from the up platform in about 1930. A signal box and down refuge siding were added in 1891, and these can be glimpsed beyond the road bridge. The up refuge siding was located behind the camera.

   Closure came on 4 June 1971, with the signal box surviving until the following January. In this more elevated view, Class 47 No 47805 passes the site of the station on 3 May 1996 with the 12.17 Manchester to Plymouth CrossCountry service. *Brunel University, Mowat collection/DHM*

HIGHBRIDGE WEST (1) was one of the original stations when the broad gauge B&E opened as far as Bridgwater on 14 June 1841. When the Somerset Central opened its line from Highbridge Wharf to Glastonbury, it crossed the B&E on the level. In this view from 1 January 1966 the LCGB's 'Mendip Merchantman' tour has just traversed this crossing (visible on the left, and which by this date gave access only to the former GWR goods yard), and is now standing in the rain in the down platform of the B&E station. Standard '9F' 2-10-0 No 92243 has been attached to haul it to Mangotsfield and Bath.

The crossing was removed when a new connection was created to serve the roadstone terminal (see page 20). Highbridge is still served by Regional Railways services and on 13 June 1996 Sprinter No 158838 calls with the 16.20 Bristol to Paignton. *Hugh Ballantyne/DHM*

HIGHBRIDGE WEST (2): Highbridge Crossing signal box is pictured on 28 June 1971 with Class 35 diesel-hydraulic No 7017 standing on the site of the flat crossing. The 'Hymek' has been engaged in shunting activity after bringing in the Bason Bridge milk train. The new junction can be observed just beyond the brake-van.

The signal box closed in the following March and was subsequently demolished. The 12.03 Newcastle to Plymouth HST speeds past on 13 June 1996. *John Medley/DHM*

DUNBALL station opened in 1873 and had staggered platforms. The down one is passed at 3.20 pm on Saturday 20 September 1947 by 'Castle' Class 4-6-0 No 5033 *Broughton Castle*, which is hauling the second part of a down Manchester to Paignton train composed of LMS stock. The line leading away to the left runs to Dunball Wharf on the River Parrett, and had its origins in a private tramway opened in 1844. In the foreground a siding to a cement works crosses the main line on the level.

The siding was removed in 1958, the station closed on 5 October 1964, and the wharf branch was taken out of use in 1967. On 13 June 1996 Class 47 No 47847 passes with the 12.17 Manchester to Plymouth. The M5 is just to the right and the landscape was changed when the motorway was built. *Pursey Short/DHM*

BRIDGWATER (1): The initial terminus of the B&E was a prosperous and expanding town, and new docks had opened shortly before the railway's arrival. A horse tramway connected the station to a wharf on the Parrett from 1845, and this was later converted into a mixed gauge line operated by locomotives. The station is pictured here looking to north in about 1930. The goods yard and docks line are to the left beyond the up platform.

The station is listed and has recently undergone substantial restoration. The docks branch closed in 1967 but a short section adjacent to the goods yard remains as a loading point for irradiated nuclear fuel from Hinkley Point power station. On 23 May 1996 Class 31 Nos 31275 and 31203 are arriving with the 17.21 (WO) empty flasks from Sellafield. *Brunel University, Mowat collection/DHM*

BRIDGWATER (2): A Paddington to Taunton train departs in 1938 behind 'Hall' Class 4-6-0 No 4945 *Milligan Hall*. The footbridge from which the previous photos were taken can be seen. Just south of here the B&E established a works that constructed most of the coaches and wagons used by the company.

The siding on the left is now disconnected and overgrown, but otherwise today's view is relatively unchanged. On 23 May 1996 'Sprinter' No 158869 departs with a Cardiff Central to Paignton service. *The late Bob Franklin/DHM*

DURSTON station was opened in 1853 as the junction with the B&E's Yeovil branch, and is seen here from the station footbridge on a very dull 16 February 1964 as 2-6-2T No 4593 and 0-6-0PT No 9663 haul 'The Quantock Flyer', an LCGB special from Waterloo, off the branch.

The station closed on 5 October 1964, a few months after the branch had closed to passengers. Its subsequent demolition prevents the taking of an exactly equivalent view, but in this scene, taken with the aid of a telephoto lens from an adjacent overbridge, we can see another double-headed steam special as Standard '4MT' 4-6-0 No 75014 and '7MT' 4-6-2 No 70000 *Britannia* head westwards on 8 April 1995. *Hugh Ballantyne/DHM*

The Somerset & Dorset: Burnham to Henstridge

BURNHAM-ON-SEA: The Somerset Central extended its line for 1½ miles from Highbridge Wharf in 1858. It was intended that Burnham would become a base for pleasure steamers with opportunities for a passenger service across the Bristol Channel to Wales, so the line continued beyond the station to run on to a pier. The railway helped the town to develop as a holiday resort, but delays to main-line trains caused by conflicting movements on the Highbridge crossing prompted the closure to passengers of this section in 1951. Excursion trains continued, however, until 1962, and one of these is pictured after arrival behind ex-GWR 0-6-0 No 2219. The scout hut on the right was formerly a lifeboat station.

Occasional goods services ran until complete closure on 20 May 1963. The scout hut survives in May 1996, but a road now runs through the station site. *David Lawrence/DHM*

HIGHBRIDGE EAST (1): The Somerset Central was built with the intention of linking the towns of Glastonbury and Street with the coast. Bridgwater was the preferred destination, but Highbridge was selected because the route of the Glastonbury Canal could be used and the line constructed more cheaply. Highbridge Wharf was about half a mile west of East station, and at 4.15 pm on Saturday 3 March 1945 S&D '3F' 0-6-0 No 3216 is returning light engine to the shed after leaving its goods train there. It has just passed Highbridge East 'B' signal box - note the GWR horse and cart waiting at the level crossing. On the right 0-6-0 No 2230 is shunting in the GWR goods yard.

A far less interesting scene on 13 June 1996 includes a Class 150/2 'Sprinter' forming the 16.22 Taunton to Gloucester service. *Pursey Short/DHM*

HIGHBRIDGE EAST (2) was provided with five platforms, but with little in the way of shelter for passengers. On a wet 5 December 1964 (*left*), Collett 0-6-0 No 3200 has arrived with the 1.15 pm from Evercreech Junction, while Ivatt 2-6-2T No 41242 stands with the 2.20 pm departure to Templecombe. In the right background are the engine shed and S&D works, the latter largely disused since closure in 1930.

The station closed in 1966, but construction of the M5 motorway in 1971 required that 750,000 tons of fly ash be brought from Aberthaw power station to a terminal adjacent to its site and a new spur was laid from the main line. The remains of Platform 5 can be seen on the right on 28 June of that year (*below left*) as English Electric Type 3 Nos 6991 and 6957 (currently 37419 and

37668 respectively) draw their train past the unloading point. This telephoto lens shot also includes the old works building on the right.

The May 1996 scene (*above*) shows that since final closure the station site has been levelled. A furniture manufacturing company occupies the shed and works area.

The final view gives a closer look of the shed on 22 May 1965 with ex-GWR 0-6-0 No 3205 standing outside.
Peter Gray/John Medley/DHM/Terry Nicholls

BASON BRIDGE station opened in July 1856, but the location grew in importance when a milk factory was established in 1909. This generated significant traffic for the railway, and also ensured the survival of the line from Highbridge for a few more years after most of the Somerset & Dorset had closed. On 28 June 1971 Class 35 No 7017 passes the station's decaying single platform with the 16.30 milk train to Taunton; the dairy is visible in the left background.

The M5 breached the railway and brought about its final closure from 3 October 1972. The platform survives, but was very overgrown when visited on 25 May 1995. The dairy was modernised after closure of the railway, but it too closed in 1987 and the buildings now form part of a business park. The 'Hymek' was withdrawn in 1975 but has been preserved and is based on the West Somerset Railway. *John Medley/DHM*

SHAPWICK station was situated over 2 miles north of the village in the heart of the Somerset levels and in one of the largest remaining wetlands in Britain. This view looking west was taken from the signal box in May 1961. The Somerset Central was originally broad gauge and the space between the tracks illustrates this fact.

The station site has been cleared since the closure of most of the S&D system on 6 March 1966. Only the widened Sedgemoor South Drain on the right provides a link on 3 May 1996. *Stations UK/DHM*

ASHCOTT: Commercial exploitation of the substantial peat deposits in the levels began in about 1870 and provided a major source of revenue for the railway. About half a mile west of Ashcott station a siding served the Eclipse Peat Company's works, and a 2-foot-gauge tramway to the peat beds crossed the S&D on the level. On 23 October 1965 a party from the RCTS West of England branch 'grice' the tramway.

This area is known as Shapwick Heath and is now a National Nature Reserve. Peat-cutting and drainage have extensively altered the peat bog and work is now in hand to restore water levels and encourage wetland wildlife. A track follows the course of the S&D, and the bridge over the South Drain leads to the site of the Eclipse works, which has all but disappeared. *Peter Gray/DHM*

GLASTONBURY & STREET (1) was the original eastern terminus of the Somerset Central. This is the eastern end of the station on 10 April 1962, with 0-6-0 No 3216 arriving with the 9.55 am Evercreech Junction-Highbridge service as 2-6-2T No 41242 waits to cross on the 9.45 am Highbridge to Templecombe. Although fostered by the B&E, the SCR was an independent company with the two towns' quaker businessmen prominent in its formation. Pressure from shareholders led to an extension in the broad gauge to Wells in 1859, but subsequently the railway was to develop southwards and join the standard gauge Dorset Central at Cole in 1863. The two companies had amalgamated in the previous year to form the Somerset & Dorset Railway.

On 13 June 1996 the station area is largely clear, but planning permission has been obtained to use the site for storage. *Ron Lumber/DHM*

GLASTONBURY & STREET (2) is seen from the signal box on 7 June 1964 with two truly S&DJR engines waiting for the token before proceeding on a Home Counties Railway Society special. The 2-8-0, No 53807, was by then the last S&D '7F' working, while the '4F' 0-6-0, No 44558, had been built for the S&D to a Midland design in 1922. Prominent on the skyline is Glastonbury Tor, a conical hill rising from the marshlands and crowned with the ruined tower of a chapel.

The station remained largely intact until demolition in 1984. However, part of the island platform canopy was saved and erected elsewhere in the town for use as a covered market. The buildings on the left and the more modern warehouse on the right remain in June 1996 to link these views. *Hugh Ballantyne/DHM*

WEST PENNARD: The mixed gauge extension from Glastonbury to Templecombe was opened on 3 February 1862, but the broad rails were little used. This station also opened on that date and was situated about 2 miles from its village on a 4-mile straight section of line. The large stone-built goods shed is prominent on 31 August 1963 as 0-6-0 No 3210 leaves with the 4.00 pm (SO) Highbridge to Wincanton train.

The site is now occupied by a transport company with the owners living in the former station master's house, while the station building is occupied by other members of the family. The gate in the foreground of the past view now stands at the entrance to the site, while the roadbridge from which it was taken has been demolished and the road realigned. Accordingly the June 1995 scene had to be recorded from a lower angle. *Hugh Ballantyne/DHM*

PYLLE (1): Ivatt 2-6-2T No 41296 departs from the station on 23 April 1960 on the 5.00 pm Evercreech Junction to Highbridge train. The 17-lever signal box had closed in 1929 when the passing loop was removed, but until 1963 the structure contained a ground frame controlling access to the small goods yard. The bridge carries the Fosse Way over the railway.

The scene on 28 June 1995 includes all of the extended goods shed, which saw use as a meat-packing plant after closure of the railway, but which at this time was being converted into a house. *Hugh Ballantyne/DHM*

PYLLE (2): The eastern end of the station on 21 August 1958 sees S&D '3F' 0-6-0 No 43194 arriving with the 2.20 pm Highbridge to Templecombe train. The goods shed, just visible on the extreme right, was most unusual as it incorporated the station master's house at this end.

The station building is also now occupied as a dwelling, and sections of the platforms still survive. The present-day photo was taken from the embankment of the widened A37. *Hugh Ballantyne/DHM*

EVERCREECH JUNCTION (1) was known simply as Evercreech when it opened in 1862, but was re-named 12 years later when services commenced over the Bath extension and Evercreech New opened. The tall South signal box controlled the level crossing over the A371, and on 14 September 1959 it is passed by ex-LMS '2P' 4-4-0 No 40652 and '5MT' No 44814 as they leave with the down 'Pines Express'. Unless hauled by one of the heavy freight engines, all trains of more than eight coaches had to be piloted during the hard climb over the Mendip

Hills, and the assisting engines were attached or detached here. On this occasion the load appears to have justified the pilot working forward to Bournemouth.

The signal box has been demolished, but the station building survives as a dwelling in April 1996.
Peter Gray/DHM

EVERCREECH JUNCTION (2): The goods yard is obscured by exhaust on 1 January 1966 as Standard '4MT' 4-6-0 No 75072 departs on a Bath train. It will shortly be taking a sharp curve at a maximum of 25 mph before heading north. Behind it a plume of smoke rises from a Highbridge train waiting on the middle road to follow this departure. The main marshalling yard is behind the camera.

Today much of the site is occupied as a private industrial estate. The goods shed is visible beyond the bow of the boat, and the old Railway Hotel is located in the distant right of both views. *Peter Gray/DHM*

COLE: It was just north of here that the Somerset Central and Dorset Central railways met, and Cole was a typical example of a DCR station. Unfortunately, however, it is lost in the smoke in this 13 March 1965 scene as Standard '4MT' 2-6-4T No 80147 makes a spectacular departure on the 4.13 pm from Evercreech Junction to Bournemouth. It is crossing the 4.15 pm Templecombe to Bath hauled by No 80043, the rear of which is just visible next to the signal box.

The formation in the foreground has been backfilled, but the bridge parapet survives and allows a similar viewpoint on 14 May 1996. The station building is a dwelling and work has commenced on additional housing in the foreground. *Peter Gray/DHM*

BETWEEN COLE AND WINCANTON: The railway passed along a straight section near the village of Shepton Montague and ran under this unusually tall bridge, known as Rock Cutting bridge, which carried the road to Stoney Stoke. Standard '4MT' No 76019 passes with the 3.20 pm Bath to Templecombe train on Whit Monday 18 May 1964.

The bridge survives, but undergrowth in the cutting dictated that this more head-on photo be taken on 4 April 1996 by standing on the boggy trackbed. *Michael Mensing/DHM*

WINCANTON: The platforms here were staggered, with that on the up side about twice the length of the down one. On 19 April 1965 Class '2MT' 2-6-2T No 41296 is standing at the latter on the 2.20 pm Highbridge-Templecombe train. The short overlap of the platforms is apparent, together with the concrete footbridge that linked them. This was added by the SR and replaced an earlier lattice bridge. The signal box was located on the up platform, just behind the camera.

A visit on 1 August 1995 revealed that a housing estate now covers the station site. However, the signal box foundations survive and helped in aligning the 'present' photo. *Ron Lumber/DHM*

TEMPLECOMBE: Just north of Templecombe No 3 Junction the railway passed under a road overbridge near the village of Horsington. On 13 August 1964 Standard '5MT' No 73054 heads south on what is probably the 4.10 pm Bath to Templecombe train.

The bridge still stands in 1996, and even 30 years after closure the formation is fairly easy to identify, albeit heavily overgrown in the foreground. *Terry Gough/DHM*

TEMPLECOMBE SHED: Once an important junction between the S&DJR and the LSWR, this bleak view shows the S&D on 4 June 1967 in its final days. It is over a year since the last passenger train ran and all the track has been removed other than the main running line, over which North British Type 2 (later Class 22) No D6337 is heading south with a demolition train en route to Sturminster Newton, which was the railhead at that time. The original Dorset Central station buildings are still standing, however, along with three more modern structures including the 1950-built engine shed. In the right distance Templecombe No 2 Junction signal box is visible and the course of the line to Templecombe Upper can be followed from there to the left.

The April 1996 view shows the site occupied by the Sonar Systems Division of GEC Marconi Underwater Systems. The modern railway buildings have survived, however, including the engine shed. *Hugh Ballantyne/DHM*

HENSTRIDGE was the smallest station on the line with a single platform about 150 feet long. It is passed on Sunday 6 March 1966 by an SLS 'last day' special hauled by LMS '8F' 2-8-0 No 48706 and Standard '4MT' 2-6-4T No 80043.

The May 1996 view shows that the level crossing gatepost and the distant overbridge both survive, but in between the station has been swept away with recently erected housing on the left. *Peter Gray/DHM*

The Somerset & Dorset: Evercreech New to Chilcompton

EVERCREECH NEW: The S&D endured a number of financial crises and the company considered that a profitable solution would be to drive northwards and provide a link between the Midlands and the South Coast. The Bath extension was therefore built, and was to become the main line, with the original route from Highbridge becoming a branch. However, completion of the extension financially exhausted the company and in 1875 an agreement was signed whereby the Midland Railway and the LSWR would jointly lease the line. The first station on the extension Evercreech New, was located on the edge of the village. On Saturday 21 July 1962 it is passed by Standard '9F' 2-10-0 No 92210 which is hauling the 12-coach 9.25 am Bournemouth West to Liverpool and Manchester train.

Housing now covers the site, but original railings from the up platform survive on the right and provide a link with the past in June 1995. *Ron Lumber/DHM*

PRESTLEIGH VIADUCT, about halfway between Evercreech New and Shepton Mallet, was constructed of limestone. On 31 July 1965 Bath's chime-whistle Standard Class '5' 4-6-0 No 73001 crosses the viaduct on the 1 in 50 upward slog with the 3.40 pm Bournemouth West to Bristol Temple Meads service.

The viaduct survived until January 1993 but was demolished due to its deteriorating condition. Only the embankments at each end survive in June 1996 to remind us of its existence. The tree on the right has been felled and we are now allowed a clear view of the house in the valley. *Hugh Ballantyne/DHM*

SHEPTON MALLET (CHARLTON ROAD) station was provided with a fair-sized goods yard to serve this important market town and commercial centre. Additional sidings served a quarry and the railway's signal works, until the latter closed in 1930. On 15 March 1955 '7F' 2-8-0 No 53804 rattles through with an Evercreech Junction to Bath goods. This was one of six engines designed specially for the S&D by Sir Henry Fowler and built at Derby in 1914. So successful were they that five similar locos, but with larger boilers, were built by Robert Stephenson & Co in 1925. Final withdrawal did not occur until 1964 and fortunately two of the class are now preserved.

An industrial estate now covers this site, and the house on the extreme left is the best reference point when comparing these views. *Hugh Ballantyne/DHM*

WINSOR HILL TUNNEL: The original 239-yard tunnel was used by down trains after the line was doubled in 1892. The new up bore was only 126 yards long thanks to a slight deviation that reduced construction costs. On 4 May 1963 Standard '5MT' 4-6-0 No 73049 has just emerged from the latter bore with the 3.40 pm Bournemouth West to Bristol Temple Meads train. The sidings on the right had served the closed Ham Wood Quarry. Another quarry, Winsor Hill, was located to the left of this scene. The stone-built signal box, which is partly obscured by exhaust, had controlled access to the sidings.

The undergrowth hides the tunnel portals, but both are in good condition and used by walkers. At the time of this 1995 visit there were proposals to create a Chinese Garden in the area with finance from the Millennium Fund. *Michael Mensing/DHM*

MASBURY station opened with the line, but became an unstaffed halt from 1938. On 21 July 1962 Standard '4MT' 4-6-0 No 75073 passes with the 12.03 pm Templecombe to Bath train. The smoke is hiding the large station master's house, but the small goods yard can just be noted behind the train. Sidings on the down side were provided to serve a US Army camp during the Second World War, but these had been lifted in 1959.

The station is now occupied as a private residence. Trees were planted in the trackbed after closure and even on 4 April 1996, before the summer foliage has appeared, the same view today is largely obscured. *Ron Lumber/DHM*

MASBURY SUMMIT (1): At 811 feet above sea level this was the limit of the S&D's climb of the Mendips. On 1 September 1962, the penultimate Saturday of through trains over the route, '7F' No 53810 passes the summit and approaches Oakhill Road bridge after its 1 in 50 climb from Masbury station with the Exmouth and Sidmouth to Cleethorpes train. Although designed as a freight engine, this class often appeared on such summer Saturday workings from 1950.

The roadbridge has been demolished and the cutting on both sides filled in and levelled. The deeper section of the cutting in the distance is gradually becoming overgrown. *Hugh Ballantyne/DHM*

MASBURY SUMMIT (2): Looking in the opposite direction on 4 May 1963, Standard '5MT' 4-6-0 No 73054 approaches the road bridge having almost completed the northerly climb to the summit with the 3.35 pm Bristol Temple Meads to Bournemouth West train.

The levelled formation has been assimilated into the field. On 12 July 1995 only the tree on the extreme left and the line of trees in the background provide reference points when comparing these scenes. *Michael Mensing/DHM*

BINEGAR (1): Also on 4 May 1963, LMS '4F' 0-6-0 No 44411 rolls down from Masbury Summit with the 4.15 pm Templecombe to Bath Green Park train. With less than a mile to go to Binegar station, it is about to cross Binegar Bottom bridge and the road to Wells.

The bridge still stands, but when this location was visited in the summer of 1995 it was totally hidden by foliage. A return visit was therefore made in the following April to record the present scene. *Michael Mensing/DHM*

BINEGAR (2) is a small village and the station was probably more important to the railway as a source of freight traffic. In 1903 sidings were laid to the north of the station to serve the Mendip Stone Works, while from 1904 to 1921 a 2-mile-long, 3-foot-gauge line brought the products of Oakhill Brewery to the station. At 4.40 pm on 4 March 1961 pioneer LMS '2P' 4-4-0 No 40563 is leaving on the 3.20 pm Bath Green Park to Templecombe local service.

A large dwelling and bungalow have been erected on the site of the station, but the Station House on the right is still occupied and links these views. *Peter Gray/DHM*

CHILCOMPTON station was close to the famous public school Downside, and special trains ran from here to London each term. It also featured a large water tower, which was used by banking engines returning to Radstock, and at the west end sidings were provided to serve a nearby colliery. On 5 March 1966, the last public day of service, unrebuilt Bulleid 'Pacifics' Nos 34006 *Bude* and 34057 *Biggin Hill* gleam in the winter sunshine as participants in the LCGB's S&D farewell tour take advantage of a photo stop while en route to Bath.

In July 1995 remnants of the platform could be traced, but the formation was heavily overgrown. The land to the left of these scenes was then derelict, but a further visit nine months later revealed that the site was being developed for housing with a number of dwellings already occupied. *Hugh Ballantyne/DHM*

CHILCOMPTON TUNNEL (1): On 24 July 1965 Standard '4MT' 2-6-0 No 76056 heads away from the southern end of the 66-yard-long tunnel with the 5.55 pm Bristol Temple Meads to Bournemouth West service. The train has been climbing at 1 in 53 for over a mile since leaving Midsomer Norton.
Viewed from this end in April 1996 the two bores are intact, with the up-side one used by the Midsomer Norton Rifle & Pistol Club as a range; the down-side bore is used as a storage shed. *Michael Mensing/DHM*

CHILCOMPTON TUNNEL (2): This view of the northern end emphasises the tunnel's shortness, and one wonders why the steep-sided cutting leading to the tunnel was not continued instead of boring through the hillside for this final stretch. On 4 May 1963 Standard '5MT' 4-6-0 No 73050 climbs away in the distance on the 1.10 pm Bath Green Park to Templecombe train. This engine is now preserved on the Nene Valley Railway.

The cutting has been completely infilled and the land returned to grazing. Part of the pillbox visible above the tunnel on the left survives in June 1996. *Michael Mensing/DHM*

Rails around Frome

CLINK ROAD JUNCTION signal box opened with the 2-mile-long Frome avoiding line on 1 January 1933; expresses to the West had previously been delayed by speed restrictions through the station. On 18 August 1981 Class 47 No 47342 passes the box with loaded MSV tippler wagons from Whatley Quarry. At one time there were connections to both main lines at the junction, but following a derailment in 1977 the layout was modified and the crossover next to the box installed.

   The box closed on 6 October 1984 when control passed to the Westbury panel. On 24 June 1996 Class 59 Nos 59005 *Kenneth J. Painter* and 59102 *Village of Chantry* pass with the 13.45 Merehead-Theale train. *Both DHM*

FROME MARKET SIDING: In 1854 a branch was opened from Frome to Radstock to serve the North Somerset coalfield. Passenger services did not commence until 1875, the same year that this loop siding was provided. On 29 December 1967 'Hymek' diesel-hydraulic No D7007 passes on a stone train from Somerset Quarry sidings.

The siding was taken out of use in 1968 and the site is now heavily overgrown. On 8 August 1995 ARC Class 59 No 59102 *Village of Chantry* passes with the 16.55 Whatley to Acton working. *Hugh Ballantyne/DHM*

SOMERSET STONE QUARRIES SIDING at Hapsford on the Frome to Radstock line was opened in 1895 to serve Vallis Vale limestone quarries. A narrow gauge tramway was provided to connect with the workings, but with increasing traffic this was converted to standard gauge in 1943. By this time Whatley Quarry had been opened and eventually all the crushing and processing facilities were moved there from Hapsford. On 3 April 1965 0-6-0PT No 3735 has just left the siding via the South Ground Frame with the returning Saturday pick-up goods.

Additional exchange sidings were provided at Hapsford that year, but these proved to be inadequate and eventually in 1974 a new deviation line was opened just north of here, and these sidings were closed and lifted. On 14 May 1996 Class 59 Nos 59003 *Yeoman Highlander* and 59101 *Village of Whatley* head south with the 16.55 Whatley to Acton train. *Hugh Ballantyne/DHM*

WHATLEY BOTTOM: The new line allowed BR engines access to new exchange sidings adjacent to the quarry, and these are seen on 19 August 1981 as Class 47 No 47330 arrives with a train of empties. On the right a pair of Thomas Hill 0-4-0 diesel-hydraulic shunters are propelling further empty wagons to the quarry, which is behind the camera.

Further investment by the Amey Roadstone Corporation in 1987 has transformed this view. On 6 June 1996 0-6-0 shunter *Pride of Whatley* grinds towards the quarry with the 12.23 empties from Southall. Development work has included site clearance, the diversion of a river and the building of a new road bridge. Access to the quarry is now gained by the tracks on the left, while the shunter is passing the wagon repair shop. The old engine shed, which is just visible on the extreme left of the past view, is the best comparison point. *Both DHM*

MELLS ROAD (1): The Frome to Radstock branch was converted to standard gauge in 1874 to provide a continuous link with the Bristol & North Somerset Railway, which had opened in the previous year. Originally named Mells, this station was over 2 miles from the village and was more appropriately titled in 1898. On 4 June 1954 2-6-2T No 5528 arrives from the south with the 10.50 am Frome to Bristol Temple Meads service.

The last passenger train ran on 31 October 1959, but the route remained open for goods traffic. The line from here to Radstock closed completely in 1966, but a decision to close the Radstock to Bristol section meant that all traffic was re-routed south through here two years later. This included large quantities of coal bound for Portishead power station. *Hugh Ballantyne/DHM*

MELLS ROAD (2) station opened in 1887 and became an unstaffed halt in September 1956. The line was double track from here to Radstock, and this is apparent in another 4 June 1954 scene that shows 0-6-0PT No 9628 arriving on the 10.17 am Bristol-Frome service.

The last coal train ran in 1973, but traffic to the Marcroft Wagon Works at Radstock continued until its closure in 1988. That may not be the end of the story, however, for the Somerset & Avon Railway Co was formed in 1989 with the intention of re-opening this section. In the meantime the weeds grow over the remaining single set of rails in May 1996. The sign-post and some fencing on the right link these views. *Hugh Ballantyne/DHM*

FROME station opened on 7 October 1850 after the GWR had absorbed the Wilts, Somerset & Weymouth Railway and extended it from Westbury. It is a typical Brunelian station complete with a splendid overall timber roof. On 17 August 1958 Standard '5MT' 4-6-0 No 73027 approaches with a Weymouth train. The front coaches are crossing a road overbridge.

The line was singled from Frome North to Blatchbridge Junction in August 1970. On 25 June 1996 'Sprinter' No 150219 departs with the 14.57 Weymouth-Bristol service. Note that one span of the bridge has been removed. *Hugh Davies/DHM*

The third view shows the overall roof that was in such poor condition in the early 1970s that demolition was proposed. It was, however, listed and restoration work has returned it to something like its former glory. On 24 June 1996 Class 37 No 37116 *Sister Dora* stands with the 16.33 Bristol to Weymouth train. *DHM*

FROME SHED opened in 1890 and was located just to the south of the station. It had a single road and was built of timber with a slated roof, and a brick-built office adjoining. It is pictured at 11.40 am on 7 June 1959 when six locos were on shed. A malthouse dominates the background and due to a lack of space engines were often stabled in the malthouse sidings. The broad gauge goods shed is just visible on the right.

A sub-shed to Westbury, the depot was closed in September 1963. The site is now occupied by a builder's merchant and as discovered in June 1996 the malthouse has also been demolished, although a small part of its external walls have been retained. *Peter Gray/DHM*

WITHAM (1): The railway was extended from Frome to Yeovil in 1856 as a single line, with Witham as the first crossing place. The line to here was doubled in 1875 when the station was rebuilt. It is seen here in its final days on 3 September 1966 as Class 52 No D1065 *Western Consort* passes at speed with an express from Paddington. The slate-hung station master's house can be seen on the up platform just beyond the booking office.

Closure came exactly one month later, and the station has since been demolished. The 14.33 Bristol to Weymouth service comprising 'Sprinter' No 150242 passes the site on 15 August 1996. The track layout here was modified in 1972, and the nearest rails form part of a loop for trains using the Merehead branch. *Hugh Ballantyne/DHM*

TEMPLECOMBE: Originally the S&D connected with the LSWR via a loop, which involved running in both directions over the latter's up main line. In 1870 the western curve was brought into use allowing S&D trains direct access to the upper station, but this required the use of assisting engines and reversals in both directions. On 14 September 1959 '2P' 4-4-0 No 40700 is being pulled back towards No 2 Junction by '3F' 0-6-0 No 43436 before it can continue south with the 4.16 pm Evercreech Junction to Bournemouth West train.

The bridge over the A357 and embankment have been removed, but the school on the left and house on the right remain to identify the location in July 1996. In the middle distance the road to the Marconi factory follows the course of the railway. *Peter Gray/David Mitchell*

OAKE: About 2½ miles west of Norton Fitzwarren the Barnstaple line passed under a road overbridge leading to the village of Oake. On 20 July 1963 2-6-0 No 7333 approaches the bridge with the 4.25 pm from Taunton to Barnstaple.

Not only does the bridge survive in July 1996, but also the trackbed can be easily identified even though the land has been assimilated into the adjacent field. *Peter Gray/David Mitchell*

DULVERTON station is pictured from the adjacent road bridge on 15 June 1963. The rear of the 4.10 pm Barnstaple Junction to Taunton train, hauled by 2-6-0 No 6372, can be seen standing at the up platform, while another 'Mogul', No 7304, is heading the 4.20 pm Taunton-Barnstaple service and 0-4-2T No 1421 awaits its 5.15 pm departure to Exeter St Davids.

The 28 April 1996 view shows that the main station building, goods shed and part of the up platform all still survive, with the former used as staff accommodation for the nearby Carnarvon Arms Hotel. *Peter Gray/David Mitchell*

TAUNTON: Plumes of steam rise from the engine shed at 1.12 pm on 11 August 1962, but the new order is represented by Type 4 diesel-hydraulic (later Class 52) No D1006 *Western Stalwart* as it powers the 10.30 am Paddington to Penzance, the 'Cornish Riviera Express'. The 'Western' had only been in traffic for just over two months, but was itself to be withdrawn in April 1975.

One of the classes to supplant it was the Brush diesel-electric Type 4, and on 10 July 1996 No 47787 *Victim Support* heads west through a much rationalised layout with the 12.14 Bristol Temple Meads to Plymouth empty mail vans. *Peter Gray/David Mitchell*

WASHFORD: The later days of through summer Saturday workings over the Minehead branch are illustrated on 7 September 1968 as a 12-car Inter City DMU forms the 8.50 am from Paddington. The branch's decline is evident with the derelict land on the left formerly occupied by a small goods yard.

This West Somerset Railway station is now the headquarters for the Somerset & Dorset Railway Trust, and track has been laid on the site of the goods yard for stock storage. On 17 June 1996 ex-GWR 2-6-2T No 4160 is arriving on the 16.05 Bishop's Lydeard to Minehead train. *Peter Gray/David Mitchell*

YEOVIL PEN MILL originally had an overall roof, and is also rather unusual in that although it has two platforms, the up line has faces on both sides. The up platform is also signalled in both directions, and this allowed for Taunton trains to both arrive and depart from here when the platform was not otherwise needed. However, on this occasion on 30 May 1964, 2-6-2T No 4591 is waiting at the down platform on the 12.37 pm (SO) departure to Taunton, while a DMU is forming the 11.40 am Weymouth to Westbury service.

The Yeovil area is the sole remaining outpost of semaphore signalling on the Railtrack network in Somerset. Steam also returned to the station on 9 October 1994 when, during a weekend event organised by the Yeovil Junction-based South West Main Line Steam Company, a shuttle service from here to Junction was worked by 'M7' 0-4-4T No 30053 (disguised as 30129). *Peter Gray/David Mitchell*

CHARD JUNCTION: There is much activity at the east end of the main-line station on 10 February 1962 as 'S15' 4-6-0 No 30828 approaches with the 3.34 pm Templecombe to Exeter Central train. On the left 'West Country' 4-6-2 No 34091 *Weymouth* heads the 3.20 pm Exeter-Templecombe.

Although the up platform is substantially intact, the down one has been demolished, and this, together with undergrowth, dictated that the current scene be photographed from the level crossing. On 6 September 1996 Class 159 No 159010 heads away forming the 11.30 Exeter to Waterloo service. Only about a half of the current service is booked to use the passing loop here. *Peter Gray/David Mitchell*

WHITEBALL TUNNEL is 1,088 yards long and marks the county boundary with Devon. At 1.39 pm on 9 June 1962 'Castle' Class 4-6-0 No 5071 *Spitfire* climbs Wellington bank and approaches the tunnel mouth with the 7.35 am Nottingham to Penzance relief train.

The sides of the cutting are now heavily overgrown, and a slightly different angle had to be used on 18 June 1996 to record Class 37 No 37137 on the 12.00 Westbury-Meldon Quarry ballast empties. *Peter Gray/David Mitchell*

WITHAM (2) was also the starting point for the East Somerset Railway, with branch services using a bay platform at the west end of the station. This platform was possibly unique in having a timber overall roof sufficient
to cover one carriage, with an extended canopy over part of the main up platform. This had been removed by
17 February 1962 when we see 0-6-0PT No 9668 preparing to depart on the 1.30 pm to Yatton, but one of the
roof supports has been left in situ next to the nameboard.

No trace of the station remains on 6 June 1996 as Class 37 No 37010 passes with the 10.00 Westbury to
Meldon Quarry ballast empties. *Terry Nicholls/DHM*

WITHAM (3): Dating from circa 1877 with rebuilding in 1896, the signal box was still active on 18 August 1981 as Class 37 Nos 37224 and 37210 eased off the branch with a stone train from Foster Yeoman's giant Merehead Quarry. The goods yard track in the foreground had recently been taken out of use and was awaiting removal.

The box closed in November 1984 when the area came under the Westbury panel. The site is now known as East Somerset Junction and is pictured on 14 May 1996 as Class 59 No 59004 *Yeoman Challenger* joins the up main with a long rake of bogie hoppers forming the 13.45 Merehead-Theale train. A redundant stop block stands forlornly in the former goods yard. *Both DHM*

'The Strawberry Line'

MEREHEAD QUARRY JUNCTION: The branch from Witham to Yatton ran in the vale to the south of the Mendip Hills, and towns such as Cheddar and Axbridge are protected from the north by this great limestone wall; the area basks in sunshine and local farmers specialise in growing strawberries. At one time this produced a substantial seasonal traffic for the railway and it is easy to understand how this branch acquired its nickname. Standard '3MT' 2-6-2T No 82037 passes Mitchell's Elm, between Wanstrow and Cranmore, on 5 August 1963 with the 6.20 pm Witham to Wells service.

This site was transformed in 1973 when a new chord line was opened here to provide direct access to Merehead Quarry and thus complete a triangle, with empty trains running straight into reception sidings outside the terminal. Loaded trains are propelled out of adjacent sidings on the original trailing connection with the branch. On 14 May 1996 Class 59 No 59104 *Village of Great Elm* heads towards the quarry on the 09.15 Theale empties. *Michael Mensing/DHM*

CRANMORE: The East Somerset opened from Witham to Shepton Mallet on 9 November 1858. It was worked by the GWR and thus built to the broad gauge, with conversion in 1874. Cranmore was the only intermediate station, and is seen here on 21 August 1958 as 0-6-0PT No 8744 arrives on the 3.28 pm Witham to Bristol Temple Meads train.

After closure of the rest of the branch, the section from Witham to here was retained until 1985 to serve a bitumen depot. In the meantime a preservation company founded by artist David Shepherd had established a base here, and was able to take over the whole site when the bitumen traffic ceased. This August 1996 photograph shows that unfortunately the down platform has been demolished. *Hugh Ballantyne/DHM*

NEAR MENDIP VALE: On 23 April 1960 Ivatt 2-6-2T No 41202 climbs towards Cranmore with the 2.45 pm train from Yatton to Witham.

Originally the preserved railway, also known as the East Somerset Railway, only ran for a fairly short distance to a new halt known as Merryfield Lane, but in 1985 it was extended to another purpose-built terminus known as Mendip Vale. This station is hidden behind the foliage to the right of the signal arm in this 15 August 1996 scene as Standard '9F' 2-10-0 No 92203 *Black Prince* returns to Cranmore. *Hugh Ballantyne/DHM*

NEAR DOULTING: Viewed from high ground known as Doulting Sheep Sleight, Shepton Mallet and the Mendip Hills provide a backdrop for Standard '3MT' 2-6-2T No 82035 and the 11.12 am Yatton to Witham on 21 July 1962. Much of the formation is intact in June 1996 and the course of the railway can be followed to an expanded Shepton Mallet. Mendip Vale halt is not far to the right of this scene. *Peter Gray/DHM*

NEAR SHEPTON MALLET (HIGH STREET) (1): When the S&D's Bath extension opened in 1874, it passed under the Witham to Yatton route by way of a brick-arch bridge. On doubling of the S&D in 1892 an additional metal section was provided. On 4 May 1963 another prairie tank, No 82039, crosses the S&D at the head of the 2.45 pm Yatton-Witham train. Charlton Road station can be seen immediately to the right of the engine.

The bridge survives and was being used in 1995 for storage purposes. A small industrial estate has been developed in the cutting leading to it. *Michael Mensing/DHM*

NEAR SHEPTON MALLET (HIGH STREET) (2): Less than a mile to the east of High Street station the branch crossed Kilver Street, with crossing gates controlled by a ground frame contained in the hut on the right. On 23 May 1959 2-6-2T No 82043 passes with the 2.52 pm Yatton to Witham service.

When passenger services over the branch were withdrawn on 7 September 1963, the ground frame was disconnected and the crossing gates had to be opened by the goods trains' crews. In July 1996 there is no trace of the crossing, but the telegraph pole remains and the trees in the background mark the former trackbed. Behind the camera a bungalow stands on the route of the railway, next to an extended crossing-keeper's cottage. *Hugh Ballantyne/DHM*

SHEPTON MALLET (HIGH STREET): On 23 May 1959 0-6-0PT No 5757 arrives with the 3.28 pm Witham to Bristol Temple Meads train. The suffix High Street was added in September 1949 to distinguish it from the S&D's Charlton Road station, which was so named at the same time. The GWR station was much more conveniently situated than its rival on the eastern outskirts of the town.

This area has been developed as a small industrial estate with the main station building (on the left) occupied as an engineering workshop. The road overbridge also still stands but is hidden by the trees in the background. *Hugh Ballantyne/DHM*

DULCOTE QUARRY, NEAR WELLS: The branch served a number of quarries en route and these accounted for much of the line's income. This quarry is another Foster Yeoman operation and had its own narrow gauge system, which connected with sidings to the branch, Just to the west of these on 4 May 1963, Collett 0-6-0 No 2268 approaches with the 6.15 pm Yatton to Witham service.

The branch was truncated here in 1969 with plans to develop a stone terminal, but these were abandoned in favour of Merehead. The overbridge has been demolished and the road realigned, while the cutting has been filled in and in April 1996 was being used by traffic from the quarry to nearby road works. Wells Cathedral can just be glimpsed in the background.
Michael Mensing/DHM

WELLS (TUCKER STREET): The East Somerset extended its route to England's smallest city in 1862 with a station just to the east of the S&D's Priory Road terminus. In 1870 the B&E's branch from Yatton arrived, its Tucker Street station located a few hundred yards to the west of Priory Road. Shortly after taking over the ESR, the GWR laid a connection, and eventually the ESR station became a goods depot with Tucker Street handling the passenger traffic. On 31 August 1963 '5700' Class pannier tank No 3696 stands with the 3.28 pm Witham to Bristol Temple Meads train.

A new relief road now follows the route of the railway and was nearing completion in June 1996. *Hugh Ballantyne/DHM*

WOOKEY station opened in 1871. It had a single platform, but from 1900 was provided with a loop that could be used to cross freight trains. It also had a small goods yard with rails running to a paper mill. Ex-LMS 2MT 2-6-2T No 41248 is leaving with the 1.25 pm Bristol Temple Meads to Wells service on 4 May 1963.

A visit in April 1996 found that the platform had gone, but that the goods shed still stood and was being used by an engineering company. *Michael Mensing/DHM*

CHEDDAR: A market town renowned for both its cheese and strawberries, its station was provided with two platforms and was an important crossing place on the branch. On 17 August 1963 Ivatt prairie tank No 41245 and the 3.28 pm Witham to Bristol Temple Meads train stand beneath the splendid overall roof. Cheddar Gorge and its famous caves are only a short distance away and provided tourist traffic for the branch, as indeed also did the nearby attractions of Wookey Hole and Wells.

The station site is now occupied by the stonemasons of Wells Cathedral, with the main station building surviving. Out of view on the left, the goods shed has been converted to a house. *Hugh Ballantyne/DHM*

AXBRIDGE: On 4 March 1961 0-6-0PT No 3776 enters the station with the 1.30 pm (SO) Witham to Bristol train. The western end of the Mendip Hills provides a backdrop.

On 3 May 1996 road traffic speeds along the A371 that now bypasses the town by following the route of the railway. However, behind the camera both the goods shed and main station building still stand. On the distant hillside St Michael's Cheshire Home provides a link between the two photos. *Peter Gray/DHM*

Brewham to Langport East

BREWHAM signal box stood alongside the down main line between Witham and Bruton at the summit of the steep climb from Castle Cary. The original box opened in 1907, but was destroyed by fire 40 years later. The replacement building is pictured on 18 June 1960 as 4-6-0 No 6016 *King Edward V* passes with the 1.25 pm Paddington to Kingswear express, after having nearly been brought to a stand due to adverse signals. The siding in the foreground was for bank-ing engines awaiting a path back down the bank.

The siding was taken out of use in 1963 and the box closed in October 1966. On 14 May 1996 Class 37 No 37427 *Highland Enterprise* passes with the 16.33 Bristol Temple Meads to Weymouth train. *Hugh Ballantyne/DHM*

CASTLE CARY (1): The station opened on 1 September 1856 and was provided with a passing loop on the then single broad gauge line. After conversion to standard gauge in 1874, the line from Witham to here was doubled in 1880. The eastern approach is pictured on 15 August 1981 as Class 33 No 33049 arrives with the 17.20 Cardiff Central to Weymouth service. The up and down goods loops had been added in 1943.

The signalling came under the control of the Westbury panel in February 1985 and major alterations took place as a prelude to this, including track rationalisation and the rebuilding of the down island platform so that Weymouth trains can call at either face. The up platform has also been extended. Class 37 No 37798 passes on 14 June 1996 with the 13.34 (TFO) Fawley-Tavistock Junction service conveying bitumen tanks for Plymouth Cattewater. *Both DHM*

CASTLE CARY (2) gained greatly in importance in 1906 when the new cut-off main line was opened to Taunton and it became a junction. Among the changes was the erection of a new signal box, but this was to be destroyed in September 1942 when the station was bombed. The replacement box can be seen in the distance in this 1950s view from the footbridge looking westwards.

On 11 October 1995 Class 37 No 37427 *Highland Enterprise* arrives with the 08.40 Weymouth-Bristol train. Up Weymouth trains are now routed along either side of the down island platform, then proceed along the down side for a further distance before gaining the up main via a facing crossover east of the station. *David Lawrence/DHM*

CASTLE CARY (3): Viewed from the west on 18 July 1984, Class 50 No 50038 *Formidable* speeds past the signal box and junction with the 09.40 from Paddington to Penzance. The Weymouth line had been singled in 1968, and work on rebuilding the down platform is evident in the right distance.

The signal box closed on 3 February 1985 and has been demolished. However, the goods shed still stands in commercial use, and nearby a tall radio mast is prominent next to the relay room. The realigned junction is pictured on 11 October 1995 as Class 37 No 37057 passes with the 10.00 Westbury-Meldon Quarry ballast empties. *Both DHM*

KEINTON MANDEVILLE: The GWR and LSWR had long battled for the traffic from London to Exeter and beyond, but the former's competitive position had been hindered by its greater route mileage; this was resolved by building a new section of 'cut-off' line from Castle Cary to link up with the former B&E Yeovil branch near Langport. Keinton Mandeville station opened with the line and is pictured here in its later days in a view looking eastwards. The track on the left leads to the small goods yard.

The station closed in 1962 with the signal box suffering the same fate in September 1964. The station area is now occupied as a scrap yard, and is passed by the 15.35 Paddington to Penzance HST on 15 July 1996. A building and small section of the platform on the down side survive behind the camera. *Lens of Sutton/DHM*

CHARLTON MACKRELL: The new line opened as far as here for goods traffic on 1 July 1905, and the station is recorded on 10 April 1962, exactly five months before closure. Standard '3MT' 2-6-2T No 82030 calls with the 8.55 am Taunton to Castle Cary stopper. The track layout of the goods yard and position of the signal box were virtually identical to that at Keinton Mandeville, but in this instance are out of view behind the photographer.

On 28 June 1995 there is little to suggest that a station ever existed here as an HST set powered by Nos 43016 and 43181 storms by forming the 08.45 Penzance to Paddington service. *Ron Lumber/DHM*

LONG SUTTON & PITNEY: Passenger services over the new line commenced on 2 July 1906, with this small station opening in the following year. It was actually located at the hamlet of Upton, with the two named villages a mile or so away in either direction. Despite this, traffic apparently justified lengthening the platforms in 1914. On 8 October 1952 they are passed by 'Dukedog' 4-4-0 No 9023 as it struggles eastwards with a lengthy up freight.

A comparison in freight traffic with today's operations can be made on 24 June 1996 as Class 47 Nos 47152 and 47241 head the 10.35 Exeter Riverside to Dollands Moor 'Connectrail' service conveying china clay bound for export to Gamalero in Italy via the Channel Tunnel. *Ron Lumber/DHM*

LANGPORT EAST: The town already had a station on the Yeovil branch, but was also provided with this facility on the cut-off line. On 11 April 1962 large prairie tank No 5180 is about to depart with the 3.45 pm Taunton to Castle Cary train.

The new route was built to improve the express service to the West, and the intermediate stations never really justified themselves. The local service between Taunton and Castle Cary was withdrawn on 10 September 1962 with the closure of six stations or halts, including this one. The 09.41 Penzance to Paddington HST thunders past the site of the station on 14 April 1995. *Ron Lumber/DHM*

Routes to Yeovil

SPARKFORD was one of the original stations when the Wilts, Somerset & Weymouth Railway was extended to Yeovil Pen Mill on 1 September 1856, and another of the crossing places on the then single broad gauge line. In this view from the A303 road bridge, the original broad gauge goods shed can be noted in the distance on the up side, while the signal box dating from 1877 is at the end of the down platform.

The station closed on 3 October 1966 with the signal box lasting only until 30 November. The line from Castle Cary to Yeovil was singled in May 1968, and the A303 Sparkford bypass now crosses the site. On 14 June 1996 'Sprinter' No 150232 passes by with the 14.33 Bristol-Weymouth service. *Lens of Sutton/DHM*

MARSTON MAGNA: Originally named Marston, this station gained its second platform when the line was doubled in 1881. In this undated view looking south, the tall signal box can be observed on the up side with a small goods yard opposite; the yard was extended in 1940 to serve an ammunition depot. The building on the extreme right is the Aplin & Barrett Creamery.

This station also closed in October 1966 and little remains to remind us of its existence. On 14 June 1996 Class 150/2 No 150230 speeds north on the 14.57 Weymouth to Bristol service. The station master's house stands just to the left of these views. *Lens of Sutton/DHM*

YEOVIL PEN MILL (1) was a terminus until the line was extended to Weymouth in January 1857. From the following month B&E trains used the station when a link was opened with that company's station at Hendford. Looking south from the road bridge adjacent to the station on Sunday 2 August 1959, we see 'Battle of Britain' 4-6-2 No 34110 *66 Squadron* arriving on the 9.20 am Exeter Central to Weymouth excursion. Blowing off in front of the timber-built engine shed is another Bulleid 'Pacific', No 34069 *Hawkinge*, which is waiting to back on to the train before taking it forward. The shed had closed in the previous January.

The engine shed was subsequently demolished with most of its trackwork removed by the following year; the cattle dock siding was taken out of use in February 1964. Shortly afterwards, on 13 June, 2-6-2T No 82001 approaches with the 9.45 am from Taunton on the last day of the branch passenger service.

Services to Yeovil Town ceased on 28 November 1965, but following the withdrawal of trains between Town and Junction in October 1966 a new service operated between Pen Mill and Junction until May 1968 when it was replaced by a bus. In today's much rationalised and overgrown scene Class 37 No 37408 *Loch Rannoch* approaches with the 08.40 Weymouth to Bristol train on 25 May 1995. *Ron Lumber/Hugh Ballantyne/DHM*

YEOVIL PEN MILL (2): On 16 August 1959 LSWR 'M7' Class 0-4-4T No 30131 has just passed the engine shed on the 6.32 pm departure to Yeovil Town formed of ex-LSWR 'gate' set No 373. This combination was working the intensive shuttle service between Yeovil Town and Junction that day, with a few trips also being made to Pen Mill. There was no direct service between Junction and Pen Mill until Town closed in 1966.

This section remained open until traffic to Hendford Goods ceased in May 1968. Today most of the trackbed is used as a public footpath. *Terry Gough/DHM*

YEOVIL TOWN (1): The LSWR's Salisbury to Yeovil route opened in June 1860 with trains running to the B&E station at Hendford. The joint station at Town opened a year later, and from then Hendford was relegated to goods traffic only. Mixed gauge operating took place until the broad gauge was removed in 1882. Joint operations are illustrated on 14 September 1950 as ex-LSWR 'K10' 4-4-0 No 389 and ex-GWR 2-6-2T No 5529 (in the middle of the wagons) shunt a transfer freight from Pen Mill to Junction.

The station closed on 2 October 1966, and almost 30 years later the whole area is a car park. The road over-bridge at the end of the site is still in use, however, as one remnant of former times. *Ron Lumber/DHM*

YEOVIL TOWN (2): The engine shed here dated from the 1860s and was located just south of the station. It was a lofty building of brick construction with three roads, but the site itself was cramped and its location, more than 2 miles from the LSWR's main line at Yeovil Junction, was inconvenient. Following closure of the ex-GWR Pen Mill shed in 1959, the latter's allocation was transferred here, and it is pictured towards the end of its life at 12 noon on Sunday 16 May 1965. The engines in the foreground are Nos 9754, 75005, 80039, 41283, 41290, 82035 and 80035, while behind are Nos D808 *Centaur* and 75007, the latter under repair. The water tower was erected following the transfer of WR stock, as the old tank installed in the roof had proved to be inadequate. Closure came in June 1965, although the shed continued to be used for stabling purposes until 1968. The site is now a car park. *Ron Lumber/DHM*

101

YEOVIL TOWN (3): The latter days of the railway in the heart of Yeovil are illustrated on 13 October 1966 as diesel shunter No D4021 (later 08853) works light engine from Town to Hendford Goods, after taking a transfer freight from Junction to Pen Mill. From 1965 the closed Taunton branch line terminated at the buffer stop, and a new crossover had been added from the old siding on the right.

The scene here has been transformed, but the modern building being passed by the shunter can be spotted behind the trees on the left of this April 1995 view. *Ron Lumber/DHM*

HENDFORD HALT opened on 2 May 1932 and was situated just to the west of the goods yard and site of the original B&E station. It is pictured on 12 April 1962 as 2-6-2T No 4507 pauses with the 4.00 pm Yeovil Pen Mill to Taunton service. Close by is the vast works of Westland Aircraft.

The site of the halt has been erased from the landscape, but a footpath follows the route of the railway to Town station from behind the trees on the right. Some of the goods yard area also survives and is easily identifiable. *Ron Lumber/DHM*

NEAR MONTACUTE: The B&E's broad gauge branch from Durston to Hendford opened in October 1853, but is in its final days in this view from the A3088 road bridge as 2-6-2T No 4593 climbs Montacute bank with the 4.25 pm Taunton to Pen Mill train on 30 May 1964.

Passenger traffic was withdrawn from 15 June that year, with total closure in the following month when the Taunton Freight Concentration Depot opened. The formation from the west of Yeovil to beyond Montacute has been converted to a road, but was itself closed during June 1996 for re-surfacing work. *Peter Gray/DHM*

MONTACUTE (1): Standard Class '3MT' No 82042 stands in the station on 18 May 1964 with the 9.45 am service from Taunton. The engine was having steaming problems and was delayed for 10 minutes for a 'blow up'. Evidence of imminent closure is provided by the missing signal arm and lifted siding in the foreground. The small goods yard had been situated behind the photographer.

Holiday traffic passes by on Good Friday 14 April 1995, and no doubt the drivers are completely unaware that the railway ever existed here. *Ron Lumber/DHM*

MONTACUTE (2): This attractive station opened in 1882 to serve the nearby village and its magnificent Elizabethan mansion. The original signal box closed in 1908 when it was replaced by a new one on the single platform; it can be glimpsed beyond the awning on 13 June 1964, the last day of passenger trains, as ex-GWR prairie tank No 4593 arrives on a Yeovil Pen Mill to Taunton service.

Again, it is traffic on the A3088 that replaces the railway on 14 April 1995. *Hugh Ballantyne/DHM*

MARTOCK station had staggered platforms, and in another last-day scene taken from the end of the up side, Standard prairie tank No 82040 is about to depart with the 12.58 pm Taunton to Yeovil train. The main station buildings and sizeable goods yard were on the down side. The signal box can be seen beyond the signal, and this also controlled the level crossing.

Although the Railway Hotel survives nearby, all trace of the station has disappeared. A long-time resident of the town advised the author in April 1995 that the house in the centre with the dark window frames marked the site of the level crossing. Industrial units stand immediately behind the camera. *Ron Lumber/DHM*

LANGPORT WEST: On 11 April 1962 0-6-0PT No 3669 is about to depart with the 4.15 pm service from Taunton to Pen Mill. As can be noted, the down platform was considerably longer than the up one, but had only a small shelter whereas the main buildings were on the up side. A large goods yard was provided beyond the cattle dock on the right.

An industrial estate occupied the site of the station in May 1995, but the road overbridge remained as a reference point. *Ron Lumber/DHM*

CURRY RIVEL JUNCTION was created in July 1906, marking the point where the new 'cut off' line from Castle Cary joined the Yeovil branch. The line from the junction to Langport West was doubled at that time, and this allowed branch trains proceeding towards Taunton to wait at the junction without blocking the way for workings in the opposite direction. This situation was recorded on 13 June 1964 as '5100' Class 2-6-2T No 4131 leaves the main line with the 4.25 pm Taunton to Yeovil train. The photographer is on the 4.00 pm Pen Mill-Taunton hauled by Standard prairie No 82040.

On 24 June 1996 Class 37 No 37098 passes the site of the junction with the 12.00 Westbury to Meldon empties. *Derek Frost/DHM*

ATHELNEY: The line from Curry Rivel passes through a low-lying area subject to flooding, and when the new main line was being built this section was raised above flood level. Immediately to the west of Athelney station is a level crossing and a bridge over the River Tone. On 30 May 1964 2-6-2T No 4591 is viewed from the signal box as it approaches with the 2.10 pm(SO) Taunton to Yeovil service. It has just come off the original line via Durston and the fireman is ready to pass the single-line token to the waiting signalman. The main line heads away to the left.

The signal box closed in April 1986 and the crossing is now protected by automatic half barriers. The bridge has been rebuilt and is being crossed by the 09.35 Plymouth-Paddington HST with power cars Nos 43022 and 43147 on 14 April 1995. *Ron Lumber/DHM*

LYNG HALT served the villages of East and West Lyng and was a somewhat basic structure with the single platform face constructed of wooden sleepers, and with a simple timber shelter. On 30 May 1964 ex-GWR '4575' Class No 4593 arrives with the 11.21 Yeovil Pen Mill to Taunton working.

All trace of the halt has now gone, but the cutting is otherwise virtually unaltered on 8 April 1995. *Ron Lumber/DHM*

The South Western main line

TEMPLECOMBE: The Salisbury & Yeovil Railway opened the section from Gillingham to Sherborne in May 1860 with a station provided for this village. The location became an important railway centre when the S&D arrived in 1862. The SR totally rebuilt its station in 1938 and the 'new' enclosed concrete footbridge can be seen on 13 August 1964 as 'S15' 4-6-0 No 30833 calls with the 4.35 pm Exeter to Salisbury train.

The station closed in May 1966, and the line was singled from Wilton in the following April. In this scene, taken from further along the down platform on 27 August 1968, BRCW Type 3 No D6573 (later 33055) and 'Warship' No D818 *Glory* approach with the 10.20 Exeter-Waterloo train.

Subsequently a local group was formed with the aim of getting the station re-opened, and their efforts were successful with a service provided from 3 October 1983. Part of the upper floor of the 1938 Art Deco-style signal box was adapted as a waiting room, with the signalman issuing tickets. In 1987 Class 50 No 50021 *Rodney* approaches with the 09.38 from Exeter to Waterloo.

Re-opening was originally for a three-year trial period only, but has proved most successful. A waiting shelter was provided in 1988 and a new building added to this in 1990, when a footbridge was also provided. On 14 June 1996 'Sprinter' No 159014 departs with the 08.35 Waterloo to Exeter St Davids service. Note that the signal has been re-positioned. *Terry Gough/Ron Lumber/Terry Gough/DHM*

NEAR TEMPLECOMBE: About 1½ miles west of Templecombe, at Stowell, 'West Country' 4-6-2 No 34014 *Budleigh Salterton* hauls the 1.00 pm Waterloo to Plymouth train on 13 August 1964.

When much of the Salisbury to Exeter line was singled in 1967, a double-track section was retained from immediately west of Templecombe station to Yeovil Junction. Class 159 'Sprinters' replaced locomotive-hauled trains over this route in 1993, and on 12 May 1996 two sets, Nos 159013/009, form the 11.35 Salisbury to Exeter service. *Terry Gough/DHM*

MILBORNE PORT station was photographed from an up train on 13 August 1964, and a good view is obtained of the 1875-vintage signal box and main station building. A small extension to the box is apparent, having been constructed in 1960 to allow tickets to be purchased from the signalman.

The signal box closed in June 1965, with the demise of the station coming in the following March. The station building is now a dwelling, but 'window hanging' from modern coaching stock is impossible and prevents an exact facsimile view. *Terry Gough/DHM*

SUTTON BINGHAM: From just beyond Milborne Port the railway enters Dorset, and we re-join the route west of Yeovil Junction (see *British Railways Past and Present* No 29) at this station. In this view from the small goods yard on 29 May 1950, 'Battle of Britain' 'Pacific' No 34055 *Fighter Pilot* is approaching at speed on a Waterloo to West of England express.

The station became a halt in August 1960 and closed completely on 31 December 1962. Class 159 No 159020 passes by with the 12.58 Waterloo-Paignton service on 12 May 1996. *Pursey Short/DHM*

CREWKERNE (1): This station opened with the line and was photographed in 1933 from the road bridge that straddles the site. In the foreground can be seen part of the station footbridge, while the small signal box stands on the up platform with the goods yard beyond.

The signal box was replaced in 1960 and, although closed in 1967, the new building is still standing today. It can be observed behind the first two coaches of the 13.15 from Waterloo to Exeter as it arrives behind Class 50 No 50029 *Renown* on 19 September 1991. *Brunel University, Mowat collection/DHM*

CREWKERNE (2): North British Type 2 diesel-hydraulic (later Class 22) No D6321 approaches the up platform during the afternoon of 29 June 1966 with two brake-vans in tow.

The line from Yeovil Junction to Pinhoe, near Exeter, was singled in 1967 with crossing places provided at Chard Junction and Honiton only. The route is currently a popular and successful one, but this short-sighted measure is now hindering prospects of increasing what is basically a two-hourly service, other than in peak periods, during the day. Crewkerne station is still open and acts as a railhead for a large rural area. On 12 May 1996 Class 159 No 159011 enters the station with the 17.25 Exeter to Brighton. *Tony Wardle/DHM*

HEWISH GATES signal box controlled a level crossing over a minor road just to the west of Crewkerne. It was closed in 1967 with a colour light indicator then controlling the crossing. On 27 August 1968 Class 42 'Warship' No D820 *Grenville* approaches on the 14.35 Exeter to Waterloo train. Visible on the left are the remains of both the down main line, and the down loop that had been added in 1942 as a wartime measure.

Subsequently automatic half barriers have been installed. On 8 May 1996 Class 159 No 159017 approaches on the 11.30 Exeter to Waterloo service. *Ron Lumber/DHM*

CHARD JUNCTION (1) opened with the line in 1860 when it was known as Chard Road. A branch to Chard was later opened and the canopy for the separate branch platform can be noted just to the left of the signal box as 'H15' 4-6-0 No 476 calls with an Exeter to Salisbury stopping train on 8 July 1947.

The station closed in 1966 but the signal box was retained to control the passing loop and level crossing. The crossing gates were replaced by barriers in 1968 and the box was rebuilt in 1982. On 8 May 1996 Class 159 No 159018 passes with the 08.35 Waterloo to Exeter service. A large creamery stands just to the left; milk traffic ceased in 1981 but at the time of writing there are indications that this could be revived in the near future. *Roger Venning/DHM*

The Chard branch

CHARD JUNCTION (2): The LSWR's 3-mile-long standard gauge branch to Chard Town opened on 8 May 1863, and the branch platform is pictured on 10 February 1962 as 2-6-2T No 5554 awaits its 12.45 pm departure to Chard. The platform awning had been removed by this time, but the main-line station buildings can be seen on the right. There was no direct connection between the two lines.

The Chard Road Hotel can be seen in the background of the past view; now known as The Three Counties Inn, it provides the best reference point in May 1996. A coal yard occupies the area to the left. *Peter Gray/DHM*

CHARD CENTRAL (1): The B&E opened its broad gauge branch from Taunton to Chard Joint in September 1866. Its station was half a mile north of the LSWR station and the latter built a connecting spur with trains continuing to use the old terminus before backing out and proceeding over the spur. Chard Joint was renamed Central in 1949. 0-6-0PT No 3787 with the 3.20 pm Taunton-Chard Junction train stand beneath the handsome overall roof on 10 February 1962. The train carried a special party of RCTS members, hence the small nameboard on the centre lamp-iron. There was once a bay platform on the left for LSWR standard gauge trains, with mixed gauge over the through road.

On 8 May 1996 the buildings are substantially intact with their modern usage readily apparent from the photograph. *Peter Gray/DHM*

CHARD CENTRAL (2): The two companies operated independently of one another until after the gauge conversion in 1891. Subsequent closer co-operation culminated in the GWR working the whole branch from 1 January 1917, with Chard Town becoming the main goods depot. In another scene from 10 February 1962 we see the northern end of Central and prairie tank No 5554 on the 1.35 pm to Taunton. On the right, pannier tank No 9608 stands in the original broad gauge bay before working the 1.52 pm (SO) to Chard Junction. The tall building beyond is an animal feed processing plant.

The station and mill buildings can just be detected in today's cluttered scene. *Peter Gray/DHM*

DONYATT HALT was opened on 5 May 1928; located in a shallow cutting, it had a single platform faced with timber sleepers and a simple wooden shelter. At the top of the cutting is a line of concrete defence emplacements installed during the Second World War.

Although it was no surprise to find the concrete 'teeth' still in place in May 1996, the presence of some of the platform sleepers still in situ was not anticipated. *Author's collection/DHM*

ILMINSTER was one of the original stations on the B&E branch. It had only a single platform, but a loop was provided to allow goods trains to cross. The single-storey brick-built station building stands to the right of 0-6-0PT No 3669 and the 2.50 pm train from Taunton to Chard Central on 2 July 1956.

The area is now an industrial estate and the station building is used for storage purposes. Behind the camera, the large goods shed has also been converted for further use. *Hugh Ballantyne/DHM*

ILTON HALT opened on 26 May 1928 and was of a more substantial concrete construction. It was, however, only provided with a single seat and was without shelter for intending passengers. The two stanchions were for hanging oil lamps.

The last passenger trains ran over the branch on 8 September 1962, but goods traffic survived until 1966. No trace of this halt remains today, although the pill box located at the far end of the platform survives, hidden by the undergrowth. *Lens of Sutton/DHM*

The Taunton area

COGLOAD JUNCTION: To ease congestion, particularly on summer Saturdays, the track from Cogload Junction to Norton Fitzwarren was quadrupled, the work being completed in 1932. The down line from Bristol now used a flyover at Cogload and was thus independent of the Castle Cary line; the flyover can just be seen in the distance on 15 August 1981 as Class 45 No 45049 *The Royal Marines* heads west with the 09.45 Nottingham-Paignton service.

The section from Cogload to Taunton East Junction was reduced to double track in March 1986, with the signalling from Durston and Athelney westwards soon to come under the Exeter panel. On 23 September 1995 another 'Peak', No D172 *Ixion* of the Class 46 variation, heads Pathfinder Tours' 'Cornishman' to Penzance. *Both DHM*

TAUNTON (1): The original B&E station was rebuilt in both 1868 and 1931. The latter reconstruction retained the original down platform, but also provided both an island and a new up through platform. On 7 July 1951 Churchward 2-8-0 No 4706 stands at the island at the head of the 1.25 pm Paddington to Kingswear train. Due to the track arrangement at Cogload, trains to and from London tended to use this platform, with Bristol trains using the outer roads.

The island platform was taken out of use in March 1967, but the tracks remain in situ for non-stop services. On 13 June 1996 the 13.05 Exeter to Paddington HST is departing as in the far distance Class 47 No 47848 approaches on the 09.10 Liverpool to Plymouth train. *John Bamsey/DHM*

130

TAUNTON (2): The station was a hub for a number of branch services and five bay platforms were provided in the 1931 rebuilding in addition to the four through ones. At 11.42 am on 11 August 1962 2-6-0 No 7326 will shortly be departing from the double-faced Platform 3 with the 11.45 am to Barnstaple Junction. Meanwhile the spotters' attention is drawn to 'Hall' 4-6-0 No 4917 *Crosswood Hall* on the 10.18 am Newton Abbot to Bradford train. West signal box can be glimpsed just beyond the 'Mogul', one of five boxes then controlling signalling in the station area.

The boxes were closed progressively from 1963 to 1987 due to a combination of track rationalisation and finally the building of the Exeter Power Box. Today's simplified layout is pictured on 13 June 1996 as a 'Sprinter' departs with the 11.55 Cardiff to Penzance service. *Peter Gray/DHM*

TAUNTON (3): Fine views of the west end of the station area can be obtained from Forty Steps footbridge. On Friday 13 September 1963 the photographer was lucky to be able to record 2-6-0 No 6346 departing on the 1.15 pm train to Barnstaple Junction. The sizeable engine shed is in the right background, while the two lines on the right comprise the goods loop provided in 1896 to bypass the station.

The engine shed closed in 1964 and the track layout today is the result of work completed in May 1986 in connection with the re-signalling. On 13 June 1996 Class 37 No 37079 is heading east along the down relief line having just collected 12 cement wagons from long-term storage in Fairwater Yard. *Derek Frost/DHM*

TAUNTON (4): Forty Steps bridge can be seen in the background as Hawksworth 'County' 4-6-0 No 1020 *County of Monmouth* approaches Fairwater bridge with the 3C16 9.00 am Bristol to Plymouth parcels on 13 September 1963. The rails on the right lead to West Yard, with West Junction signal box just out of view on the left.

The yard closed in 1965 and currently the only track visible apart from the main running lines is the down relief and a section of one of the goods loop lines that remains as a headshunt for Fairwater Yard. Today's nearest equivalent train, the 12.14 Bristol to Plymouth empty vans, was captured on film behind RES Class 47 No 47793 on 13 June 1996. *Derek Frost/DHM*

SILK MILL CROSSING (1): Ex-GWR 2-8-0 No 2822 of 1907 vintage approaches the level crossing with a down Class 'H' freight at 12.10 pm on 13 September 1963. The signal box is just to the left, while Fairwater Yard is in the right background. The yard had been brought into use in 1944 and from 1960 was used for track assembly.

The signal box closed in March 1987 and has been demolished, but Fairwater Yard remains and is currently mainly used for the storage of wagons. Class 37 No 37715 *British Petroleum* heads west with an engineers' crane on 13 June 1996. *Derek Frost/DHM*

SILK MILL CROSSING (2): Also on 13 September 1963, 0-6-0PT No 9663 approaches from the west with an up local goods. The coaches in the background are contained within an MOD depot; originally a sugar beet factory had stood on the site, but the War Department opened its Blinkhorn Depot here in 1941, and it was taken over by the US Army in 1944.

'Sprinter' No 150263 works the 09.40 Paignton to Bristol on 13 June 1996. Following closure of the MOD depot, the site is now occupied as an industrial estate, but without a rail connection. However, just beyond this, part of the up relief line was reinstated in 1983 to provide access to the premises of Taunton Cider. Unfortunately this traffic ceased in 1992 when it was considered by BR to be insufficient to be profitable. *Derek Frost/DHM*

NORTON FITZWARREN: This location was known as Watchet Junction when the broad gauge West Somerset Railway opened on 31 March 1862. The branch to Barnstaple opened in 1871 but it was to be another two years before a station was provided here. Following quadrupling of the main line, two island platforms were built in 1931, linked by a footbridge from which these photographs were taken. On 30 May 1964 'Mogul' No 7337 approaches with the 2.24 pm Barnstaple to Taunton train. The Minehead line curves away above the second coach, while the Barnstaple route is immediately behind the train.

The station closed to passengers in 1961, and in this much rationalised scene on 21 May 1996 Class 37 No 37242 passes with up ballast empties. The track on the right continues from the Taunton Cider siding and allows access to the West Somerset Railway for special workings and stock transfers. *Ron Lumber/DHM*

The Minehead branch

BISHOP'S LYDEARD is seen from the adjacent road bridge on 20 July 1963 as Standard '3MT' 2-6-2T No 82030 passes with the 2.20 pm Minehead to Paddington. In the distance a DMU approaches forming the 3.25 pm service from Taunton. The section from here to Norton Fitzwarren had been doubled in 1936.

The branch closed on 4 January 1971, but a new West Somerset Railway was incorporated later that year and eventually services re-commenced between Minehead and Blue Anchor in 1976. After further extensions to Williton and Stogumber, trains to Bishop's Lydeard ran from 9 June 1979. This is now the southern terminus of the line, as various obstacles have prevented running into Taunton, not least of which the cost of running over Railtrack's metals. On 5 May 1996 'Manor' Class 4-6-0 No 7820 *Dinmore Manor* reverses its stock out of the station after completing its final run of the day. *Peter Gray/DHM*

CROWCOMBE station can be glimpsed in the distance as a three-car Swindon-built 'Cross Country' DMU departs with the 3.5 pm Taunton-Minehead service on 23 June 1965; diesel units had taken over most of the local services in 1962. The siding in the foreground was at one time used to transport stone from a nearby quarry, but was taken out of use with the down loop when the signal box closed in 1967.

In 1995 Standard '8P' 4-6-2 No 71000 *Duke of Gloucester* spent a working holiday on the line after arriving in the South West on a railtour. On 2 July it is seen departing with the 11.00 service from Bishop's Lydeard to Minehead. The signals indicate that a new signal box has been erected at the station with the loop restored. *Michael Mensing/DHM*

WILLITON: Ex-GWR large prairie No 4174 arrives with the 11.35 am Minehead to Taunton train on Friday 7 September 1962. This is one of the crossing places on the branch and on this occasion the train will be passing sister engine No 4143 on the 11.30 am Taunton-Minehead service. The wide gap between the tracks is evidence of its broad gauge origins.

On 5 May 1996 'Manor' Class 4-6-0 No 7820 *Dinmore Manor* arrives with the 15.26 Minehead to Bishop's Lydeard train. A new carriage shed can be seen on the left, while behind the camera a diesel shed had been erected just prior to this visit. *Derek Frost/DHM*

DONIFORD BEACH: Large 2-6-2T No 6113 nears the Bristol Channel coast on 24 August 1963 with the 8.50 am Swansea to Minehead train. A halt was opened here by the West Somerset Railway in June 1988, its platform coming from the closed Montacute station. On 7 May 1995 another prairie tank, but this time the smaller No 4561 of Churchward's 1906 design, arrives with the 13.55 from Williton to Minehead. *Peter Gray/DHM*

143

WATCHET was the original terminus of the branch, its harbour being the target both for this line and the earlier West Somerset Mineral Railway, which opened in 1857 to transport iron ore from the Brendon Hills. Given its importance, the station is rather unprepossessing, as shown in this 1950s view from the single platform. The wagons on the right are standing on the harbour sidings headshunt.

On 5 May 1996 '4F' No 44422 is arriving on the 14.00 Minehead to Bishop's Lydeard. *Norman Simmons/DHM*

BLUE ANCHOR: An 8-mile extension of the line from Watchet to Minehead was opened under the auspices of the Minehead Railway in 1874, the B&E working both sections as one continuous branch. Originally a single platform was provided here, but a second one with crossing loop and signal box was brought into use in 1904. Closure is less than six months away on 18 July 1970 as Class 35 No D7026 arrives with the 10.25 (SO) Minehead to Paddington service.

Two 'Hymeks' are currently based on the railway, but the present scene depicts another diesel-hydraulic class. On 29 September 1995 Class 52 Nos D1041 *Western Prince* and D1010 *Western Campaigner* arrive with the 12.20 Minehead to Bishop's Lydeard service during a diesel gala. *Hugh Ballantyne/DHM*

DUNSTER: As one of a number of measures intended to improve the branch, the line from here to Minehead was doubled in 1934 and a signal box was brought from Maerdy in South Wales to control the new layout. An earlier box had stood at the other end of this station, but was closed in 1926.

Minehead signal box closed in March 1966 and the double track was then signalled as two separate lines controlled by a bracket signal. The signal post has survived the subsequent removal of the box to Minehead, but has no use as the line was singled again in 1977. The 14.40 Bishop's Lydeard to Minehead DMU service departs on 17 June 1996. *Author's collection/DHM*

MINEHEAD is a popular seaside resort with the added attractions of Exmoor close by. The town benefited greatly from the arrival of the railway, and its island platform was extended in both 1905 and 1934 to cope with the
increasing traffic. On 7 September 1962 BR '3MT' 2-6-2T No 82044 is shunting the stock that will form the 1.23
pm departure to Taunton. However, that train will be hauled by ex-GWR 2-6-2T No 4143, while the Standard
will work the 1.35 pm goods.

The West Somerset Railway is now a thriving concern and is establishing a reputation as one of the premier
preserved railways in the country, particularly with its gala events. It is also able to receive trains from the
national network; one such working occurred on 5 March 1995 when Hertfordshire Railtours brought
Crompton No 33116 from Waterloo on the Ocean Liner stock. *Derek Frost/DHM*

West towards Barnstaple

MILVERTON (1): The first section of the broad gauge Devon & Somerset Railway opened between Norton Fitzwarren and Wiveliscombe on 8 June 1871. It was worked from the outset by the B&E, but was not formally taken over by the GWR until 1901. Doubling of the line to Milverton was completed in February 1937, and on this section, about half a mile east of Milverton, we see Pressed Steel 'Bubble Car' (later Class 121) No W55026 forming the 11.10 am Taunton to Barnstaple Junction service on 23 June 1965.

Dieselisation was not to save this route and closure came just over a year later on 3 October. The narrow bridge from which the past view was taken has been demolished and the site built up to allow for the lane to be widened, so a similar elevation is therefore possible in July 1996. *Michael Mensing/DHM*

MILVERTON (2) was the first station on the line and is pictured here on 28 September 1963 as 2-6-0 No 7332 departs with the 5.55 pm train from Taunton to Barnstaple Junction. It is passing the goods shed, but freight facilities here were to be officially withdrawn two days later.

The overbridge in the background carried the A361 road, but since closure it has been demolished and a roundabout constructed near the site. The road is now the B3227 and bypasses Milverton by running through part of the station area and westwards along the trackbed. *Hugh Ballantyne/DHM*

WIVELISCOMBE (1): The town can be seen in the background as Churchward 'Mogul' No 6345 leaves with the 7.55 am Ilfracombe to Taunton train on 25 July 1964. Among the many details that can be studied in this fine panorama is the station, which is located immediately above the engine, with the signal box and large goods shed particularly prominent.

In April 1996 the curving embankment is still largely intact. The main station building and goods shed also survive in commercial use, but are less obvious today with both the erection of additional buildings and the inevitable growth in vegetation. *Peter Gray/DHM*

WIVELISCOMBE (2): Another 2-6-0, No 6372, departs in the opposite direction with the 2.17 pm Taunton-Ilfracombe service on 18 August 1962. The line's original terminus was Barnstaple Victoria Road, but a connecting spur from there to the LSWR's Barnstaple Junction opened in 1887, and subsequently many trains ran through to that station, with certain services also going on to Ilfracombe; this was usually done by providing through coaches. The 'Moguls' first appeared on this line in the 1920s and became the main motive power until the end of steam working.

This cutting has been partly backfilled, but the main problem to overcome on 28 April 1996 was the heavy undergrowth, which dictated that the 'present' scene be photographed slightly to the left of the 'past' one. *Peter Gray/DHM*

VENN CROSS station was located in a cutting leading to a tunnel, with the main station building at a higher level than the platforms. It is partially obscured by exhaust on 7 September 1963 as Standard '3MT' No 82008 departs on the 8.00 am (SO) Wolverhampton to Ilfracombe train. The signal box is just visible behind the first coach; it dated from 1905 when the up platform and passing loop were opened to improve timekeeping on the single line. The station straddles the county boundary, which is between the box and the goods shed, so both the engine and photographer are actually in Devon.

The station building is now a residence, and the goods shed was also being converted to a dwelling in April 1996. The former has a Taunton post code, while the latter will have an Exeter one! *Ron Lumber/DHM*

DULVERTON: The Barnstaple line joined the Exe Valley branch at Morebath Junction before re-entering Somerset for a short section. This busy station was actually near the village of Brushford, with the town some 2½ miles to the north. Exe Valley services terminated here, and it was also a crossing place for certain Taunton to Barnstaple trains. On 25 July 1963 Collett 0-4-2T No 1451 propels two auto-coaches, forming the 7.10 pm departure to Exeter St Davids, away from the down side island platform.

The last passenger trains over the Exe Valley route ran just over two months later on 5 October, while Barnstaple services survived for a further three years. Since closure the site has been taken over by the nearby Carnarvon Arms Hotel, and most of this area has been levelled and grassed. A slightly wider viewpoint has been selected to include a portion of the truncated up platform and goods shed. *Ron Lumber/DHM*

The Wellington area

WELLINGTON (1): The B&E opened an extension from Taunton to Beam Bridge, on the main road west of Wellington, on 1 May 1843. This was a temporary terminus for exactly a year pending completion of Whiteball Tunnel and the remainder of the route to Exeter. The west end of Wellington station is depicted here on 4 August 1955 as 'Castle' 4-6-0 No 7000 *Viscount Portal* with the down 'Devonian' passes a pair of 4-6-0s, Nos 6996 *Blackwell Hall* and 5038 *Morlais Castle*, on the 12 noon Penzance to Crewe train.

The station closed on 5 October 1964. Class 47 No 47725 *The Railway Mission* approaches its decaying platforms with the 17.10 Plymouth to Low Fell mail train on 17 June 1996. *Peter Gray/DHM*

156

WELLINGTON (2): The station originally had two roads running through, but was re-modelled in 1931-2 with the platforms then served by loops, allowing expresses to overtake on the centre roads. A new signal box was opened at this time on the up platform, and this can be seen on 4 August 1955 as 'King' 4-6-0 No 6026 *King John* passes with the 3.48 pm Bristol to Plymouth parcels. The suffix 'Som' was added to the station name to differentiate it from its Shropshire namesake.

Most of the sidings here were taken out of use in December 1964, with the up loop removed in the following May. The down loop was retained as an engineers' siding. The signal box closed on 3 March 1986 and has been demolished. On 17 June 1996 Class 37 No 37715 *British Petroleum* passes with the 17.03 (MO) Westbury to Tavistock Junction tanks, conveying gas oil for traction depots in the South West. *Peter Gray/DHM*

157

WELLINGTON BANK rises for 3¾ miles, mainly at 1 in 80 to 1 in 90, before entering Whiteball Tunnel for a final stretch at 1 in 127. The bank will be forever remembered for No 3440 *City of Truro*'s descent at a reputed 102.3 mph in 1904 with a Plymouth to London mail train - the first recorded 'ton' on Britain's railways. Banking engines were kept at Wellington station to assist freight and some passenger trains, but on 4 August 1955 'King' 4-6-0 No 6029 *King Edward VIII* has no need for help as it climbs towards the tunnel on the down 'Cornish Riviera'.

No trains require assistance today and on 25 May 1996 Class 56 No 56073 *Tremorfa Steelworks* makes easy work of Hertfordshire Railtours' 'Paignton Decorator' from Paddington. *Peter Gray/DHM*

INDEX OF LOCATIONS